DATE DUE

DEC 1 1998			
NOV 2 9 1999			
APR 1 9 2001			
OCT 1 9 2004			
GAYLORD			PRINTED IN U.S.A

POLLUTING THE SEA

*First published in
the United States in 1991 by*
Gloucester Press
387 Park Avenue South
New York, NY 10016

Library of Congress Cataloging-in-Publication Data

Hare, Tony.
      Polluting the sea / Tony Hare
         p. cm. -- (Save our earth)
      Includes index.
      Summary: Examines the benefits we reap from
the oceans and the damage that oil spills, metal
poisoning, and sewage dumping cause.
      ISBN 0-531-17290-2
      1. Marine pollution--Juvenile literature. [1.
Marine pollution. 2. Pollution.] I. Title. II. Series.
GC1085.H36   1991
363.73'94'09162--dc20   90-43993
                                         CIP   AC

The publishers would like to
acknowledge that the
photographs reproduced within
this book have been posed by
models or have been obtained
from photographic agencies.

Design	David West Children's Book Design
Editor	Elise Bradbury
Picture research	Emma Krikler
Illustrator	Ian Moores

The author, Dr. Tony Hare, is a
writer, ecologist and TV
presenter. He works with several
environmental organizations
including the London Wildlife
Trust, the British Association of
Nature Conservationists, and
Plantlife, of which he is Chairman
of the Board.

The consultants: Jacky Karas is a
Senior Research Associate at the
School of Environmental Sciences
at the University of East Anglia.

Dr. David George, a marine
biologist, is a Principal Scientific
Officer at the Natural History
Museum in London and a Fellow
of the Institute of Biology. He
specializes in marine
environmental impact
assessment.

SAVE OUR EARTH

POLLUTING THE SEA

TONY HARE

GLOUCESTER PRESS

London · New York · Toronto · Sydney

CONTENTS

WORLDS OF WATER
6

PEOPLE AND THE SEA
8

HOW THE SEA IS
POLLUTED
10

OIL POLLUTION
12

OCEAN LITTER
14

SEWAGE POLLUTION
16

METAL POLLUTION
18

CHEMICAL POISONS
20

RADIOACTIVITY
22

POLLUTION HOTSPOTS
24

WHAT YOU CAN DO
26

FACT FILES
28

GLOSSARY
31

INDEX
32

INTRODUCTION

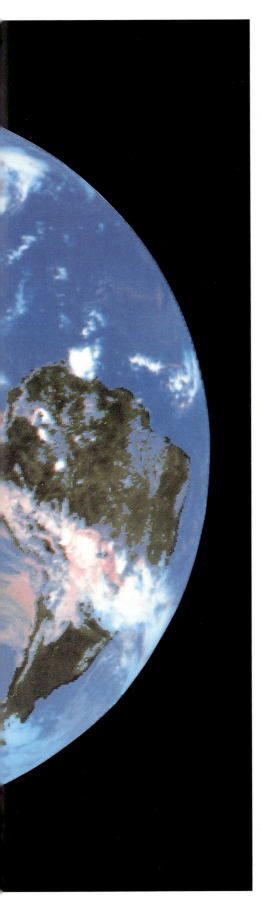

Seen from space, Earth is a watery world. Around 78 percent of the planet's surface is covered by sea. Beneath the waves there is a great variety of life, from sea plants to plankton (tiny plants and animals) to huge whales. Oceans also contain many mineral resources.

For thousands of years people have used the seas: for fishing, transportation and also for dumping waste in what seems a bottomless resource. The seas are vast, and in the past they were able to dilute and absorb the small amount of waste, mainly sewage, dumped into them. Yet now the world's increasing population produces not only huge amounts of sewage, but other natural and human-made substances. This puts serious pressure on the seas' capacity to disperse this waste.

Many of us never see the effects of ocean pollution. Yet substances like oil, plastics, sewage, industrial chemicals, pesticides and even radioactivity all harm life in the ocean. If we continue to use the oceans for unlimited dumping, we risk poisoning one of the Earth's most precious resources.

◀ **This satellite photograph shows only part of the immense Pacific Ocean. From this distance the sea does not appear to be polluted. Some sea pollution is visible at closer range, such as oil slicks and litter. But many of the pollutants that end up in the sea, like radioactivity and pesticides, are invisible.**

WORLDS OF WATER

The sea is a living world. Plant plankton soak up the Sun's energy near the surface. Beneath the waves live animals such as fish, seals, dolphins and whales. Seabirds of all kinds dive into the water to catch fish. In the deep parts of the sea, survival is hard and the animals that live there are specially adapted to their dark environment. In shallow coastal waters, like coral reefs, the sea teems with color and life. It is estimated that as many as half a million different animal species live on the world's coral reefs. On the famous Great Barrier Reef, which lies off Australia's east coast, hundreds of different types of fish can be found in an area about the same size as a football field.

The sea is also vital to life on land. Because the seas contain over 90 percent of the Earth's water, they influence the climate. They are especially important in forming clouds which blow across the land bringing rain. Oceans also help to regulate global temperatures as warm and cold currents move around continents.

Coral reefs (below right) are sometimes called the rainforests of the sea because they are so rich in life. They occur in shallow tropical seas with plenty of oxygen. Corals are tiny animals. Each animal forms a hard skeleton of limestone around itself, and it is these skeletons which form the reef over many years. The coral reef shown below is off the coast of the Sinai peninsula in Egypt.

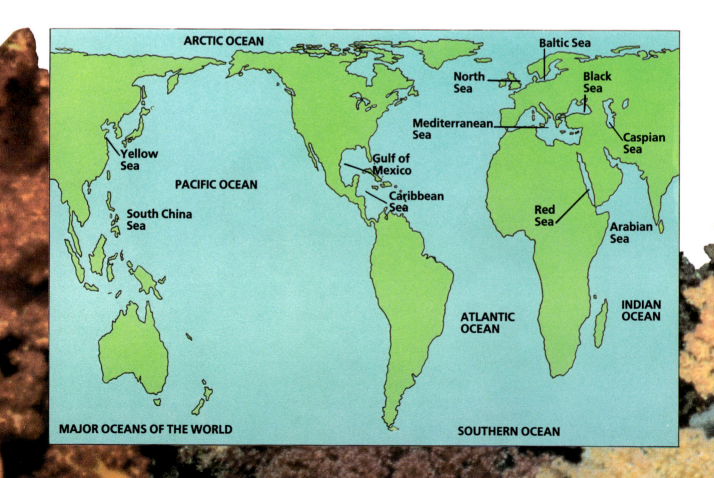

MAJOR OCEANS OF THE WORLD

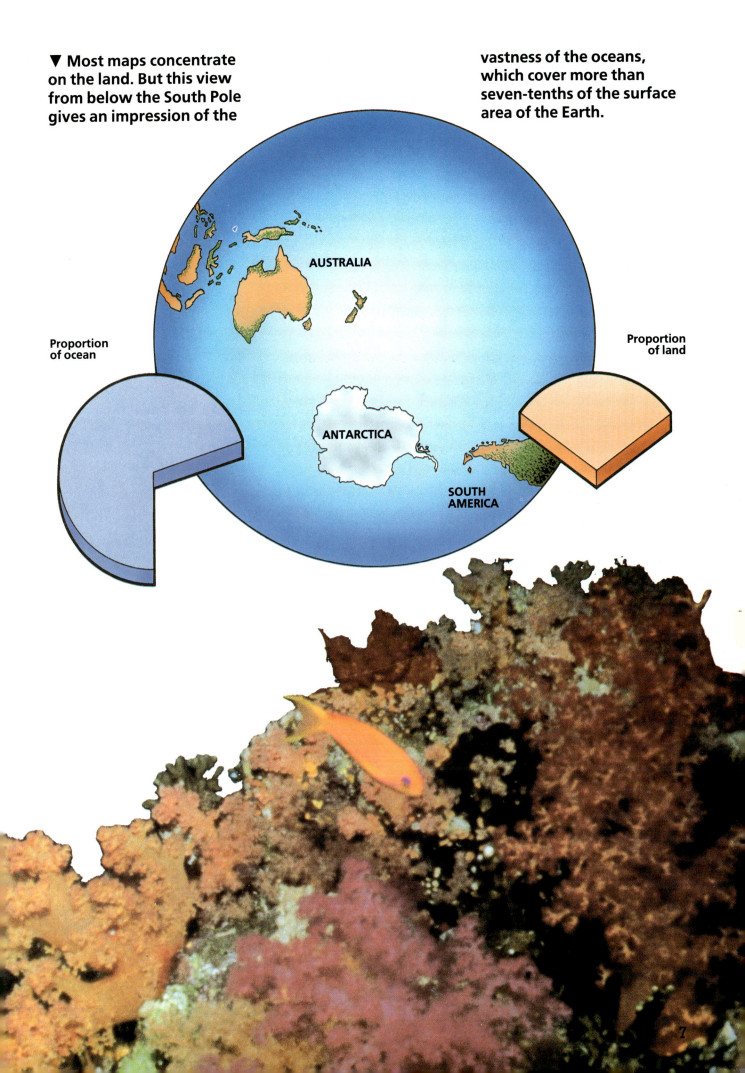

▼ Most maps concentrate on the land. But this view from below the South Pole gives an impression of the vastness of the oceans, which cover more than seven-tenths of the surface area of the Earth.

AUSTRALIA

ANTARCTICA

SOUTH AMERICA

Proportion of ocean

Proportion of land

PEOPLE AND THE SEA

More than half the world's population live on or near sea coasts. All around the coastlines of the world there are settlements, from tiny fishing villages to coastal resorts.

The ocean is full of resources. Six million tons of salt are extracted from the sea each year. Energy, in the form of oil and gas, lies beneath the seabed, and thousands of platforms pump out these fossil fuels. Most importantly, the sea provides a huge amount of food. The kinds of seafood we consume vary from great fish like tuna to tiny animals like shrimp. People in some countries, like Japan, eat sea plants. Food from the sea supplies about 23 percent of the world's protein.

If we use the sea sensibly, it will continue to supply food in the future. The growing population will need more and more food from the sea. Fish farming in coastal areas already supplies 10 percent of the world's fish harvest. But by polluting the sea we damage wildlife and we poison, or kill, our own food supply.

▶ Overfishing, as well as pollution, threatens fish supplies. Traditional fishermen, like these Malaysians (inset right), only take as much fish as they need, leaving plenty behind to breed in order to ensure future stocks. However, modern fishing methods involve taking as much fish as possible. Overfishing has devastated many fisheries, including North Sea herrings and Namibian pilchards.

Many people enjoy traveling on boats. A few compete in the great ocean races, such as the Round the World Race. But the vast majority work on fishing boats or travel on pleasure cruises and ferries as part of their vacations. There is no need for these boats to pollute the sea with garbage or oil, or damage its life, but often they do. Many countries have laws against ships' crews disposing of rubbish over the side of their boats, but these laws often do not apply in deep waters.

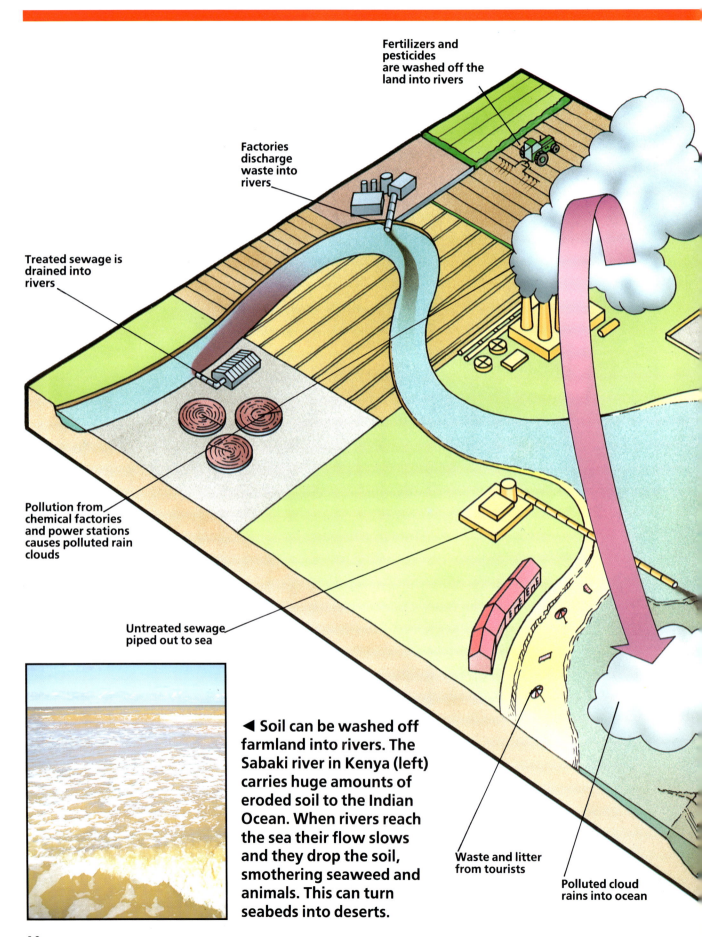

Fertilizers and
pesticides
are washed off the
land into rivers

Factories
discharge
waste into
rivers

Treated sewage is
drained into
rivers

Pollution from
chemical factories
and power stations
causes polluted rain
clouds

Untreated sewage
piped out to sea

Waste and litter
from tourists

Polluted cloud
rains into ocean

◄ Soil can be washed off farmland into rivers. The Sabaki river in Kenya (left) carries huge amounts of eroded soil to the Indian Ocean. When rivers reach the sea their flow slows and they drop the soil, smothering seaweed and animals. This can turn seabeds into deserts.

HOW THE SEA IS POLLUTED

The sea receives pollution from many sources. Ships dump sewage and other wastes directly into the sea. If ships are wrecked, their cargoes add to the pollution. Rivers carry to the sea chemicals used in farming, like pesticides which kill pests, and fertilizers which help plants grow. Soil from farms also gets washed into rivers and carried to the sea, along with poisonous wastes discharged from riverside factories. Coastal towns add their sewage and wastes from industry and power stations. Litter washes out to sea from the shores of tourist resorts. Regulations exist for some of these sources of pollution, but they are often difficult to enforce.

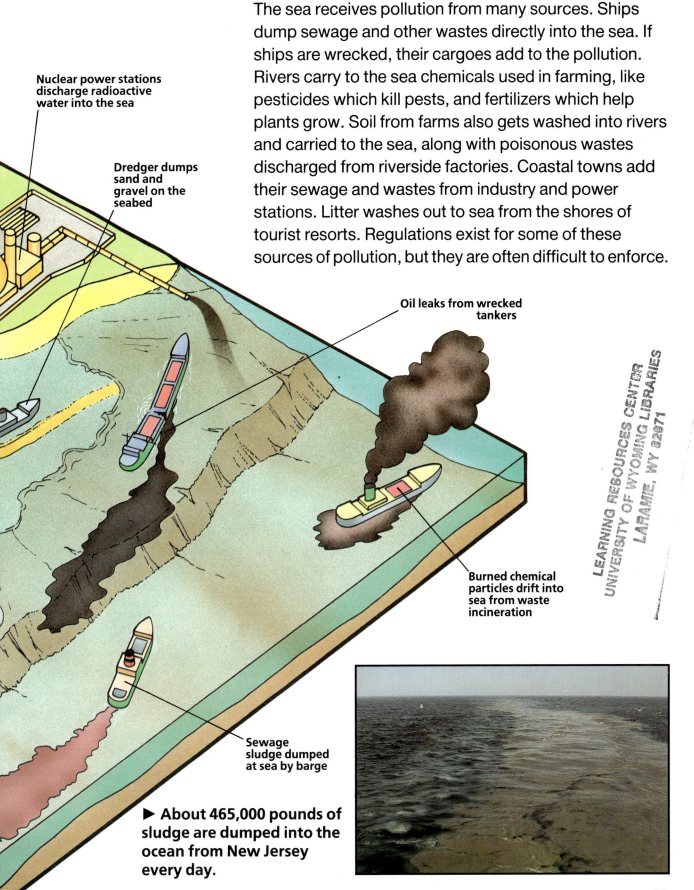

Nuclear power stations discharge radioactive water into the sea

Dredger dumps sand and gravel on the seabed

Oil leaks from wrecked tankers

Burned chemical particles drift into sea from waste incineration

Sewage sludge dumped at sea by barge

▶ About 465,000 pounds of sludge are dumped into the ocean from New Jersey every day.

OIL POLLUTION

When oil spills it covers the surface of the ocean in oil slicks which can extend over large areas. Oil can kill marine wildlife. If it washes up on the shore it ruins beaches. Oil is the best-known type of sea pollution because it is usually visible – and very damaging.

A low estimate is that about three million tons of oil a year (one tenth of one percent of the world's annual oil production) ends up in the oceans. Wrecked tankers are not the only cause of oil pollution, in fact they account for only about 10 percent of human-created oil pollution. The rest is discharged during production or from oil tankers washing out their tanks. If oily waste from cars and factories is dumped on the ground or into drains, rivers can carry it out to sea. Oil also naturally seeps from oil deposits beneath the ocean.

Oil slowly gets broken down naturally by bacteria. Oil spills can be cleaned up faster by people, but this is expensive. A better solution is to reduce oil pollution by recycling car oil and using better methods to clean out tankers' oil tanks. However, accidents still happen, so oil spills are likely to continue to make news.

▼ Today there are over 3,000 tankers on the seas, transporting half of the world's oil. Over a third of human-created oil pollution comes from transportation, through operations such as tank-washing and from accidents. Risks to shipping are greatest near coasts. So the chances are that when accidents happen, coastlines and their wildlife will be affected.

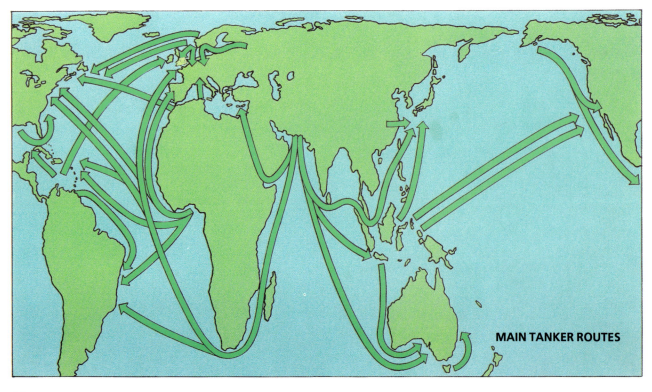

MAIN TANKER ROUTES

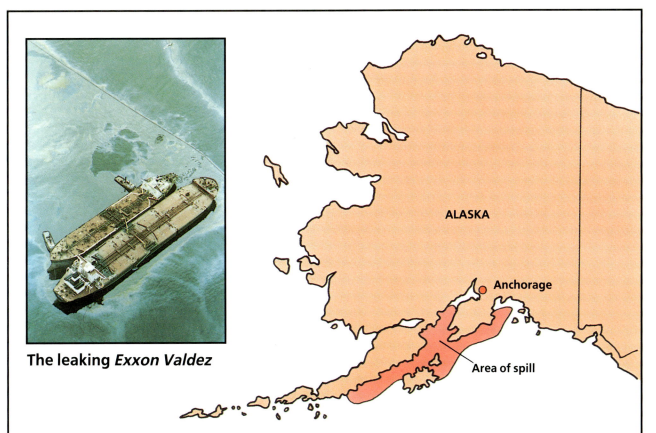

The leaking *Exxon Valdez*

ALASKA

Anchorage

Area of spill

On March 24, 1989 the oil tanker *Exxon Valdez* ran aground in Prince William Sound in Alaska. It spilled over 11 million gallons of crude oil. The effect on the local environment was devastating. Fish, seabirds and sea otters were killed in huge numbers. Otters are poisoned by oil, either by swallowing it as they swim through it or by trying to lick it off their coats. However, the main cause of death is exposure to cold. If oil clogs otters' fur they freeze to death. A few of these sea otters have been successfully rescued and cleaned. But about 3,000, along with 36,000 seabirds and over 100 eagles, are estimated to have died.

◄ This bird got caught in the oil spill from the *Exxon Valdez*. When oil clogs up a bird's feathers or an animal's fur they can no longer float. They also lose their insulation and cannot keep warm. The victims die from drowning, cold or poisoning if they swallow oil while trying to clean themselves.

OCEAN LITTER

Scattered across the surface of the sea and strewn across beaches, ocean litter is a very ugly type of pollution. It appears in many different forms, including plastic packaging, cartons, abandoned fishing nets, ropes, cans and bottles. The main litter culprits are ships' crews. Many of them throw their garbage overboard into the sea. Rivers also carry garbage from towns, and it washes into the sea from beaches.

A lot of ocean litter is made of plastic. It is estimated that 6.5 million tons of plastic are thrown off ships every year. The main problem with many types of plastic is that they decay very slowly. A plastic cup thrown from a ferry may still be in the sea 100 years later.

Ocean litter kills. Every year thousands of seabirds, fish and mammals drown or are wounded by getting tangled up in fishing nets and packaging. Others may suffer after swallowing tiny plastic balls which make them feel full and stop them from feeding properly.

▼ Litter such as bottles can often be found on beaches. Glass is dangerous to both humans and wildlife. Bottles get washed ashore after being dumped at sea, and others are left on beaches by tourists.

► The metal object trapped on this Canada goose's beak may make feeding difficult. Plastic rings that hold six-pack cans together can also be dangerous or even fatal to marine wildlife which get them caught around their necks and bodies. Some manufacturers are starting to put their cans into cardboard cartons instead of using plastic rings.

▲ Lost fishing nets can drown wildlife. This Northern fur seal survived, but the net remains.

◄ This barge is carrying domestic waste to be disposed of on land. One of the problems with litter is that we do not recycle enough of it. It has been estimated that over half the domestic waste that gets thrown away as garbage could be recycled. As recycling becomes more commonplace, the amount of litter tainting both land and sea should decrease. Some 60 countries, including the United States, prohibit the dumping of household garbage in the sea under the London Dumping Convention.

SEWAGE POLLUTION

A huge amount of sewage is drained or dumped into the sea. Around nine million cubic yards each day end up in the North Sea. In Malaysia untreated sewage from Penang is discharged into the sea, raising the bacteria levels 100 times higher than those recommended for bathing beaches in the United States.

Sewage contains substances from human, household and industrial waste which can poison the environment. It also contains bacteria, viruses and parasite eggs which are harmful to human health. The bacteria can give swimmers stomach upsets or infections. In many places sewage is left untreated before it is disposed of. It can be treated to make it safer, but this is expensive. To provide a treatment plant for a city of 200,000 people costs about $50-80 million. Sewage does break down naturally, but in the process it can seriously disrupt the environment. If dumped in large quantities it can cause wildlife to die from lack of oxygen.

▼ Because sewage contains nutrients that sea plants like algae need, they are able to reproduce very quickly when sewage is dumped in the ocean. They cover the surface of the sea with algal blooms, which can clog fishes' gills. When algae colonies die their remains are whipped to foam by the waves. These algal blooms have been washed up on a beach of the North Sea, where they can cause skin and mouth irritations to people.

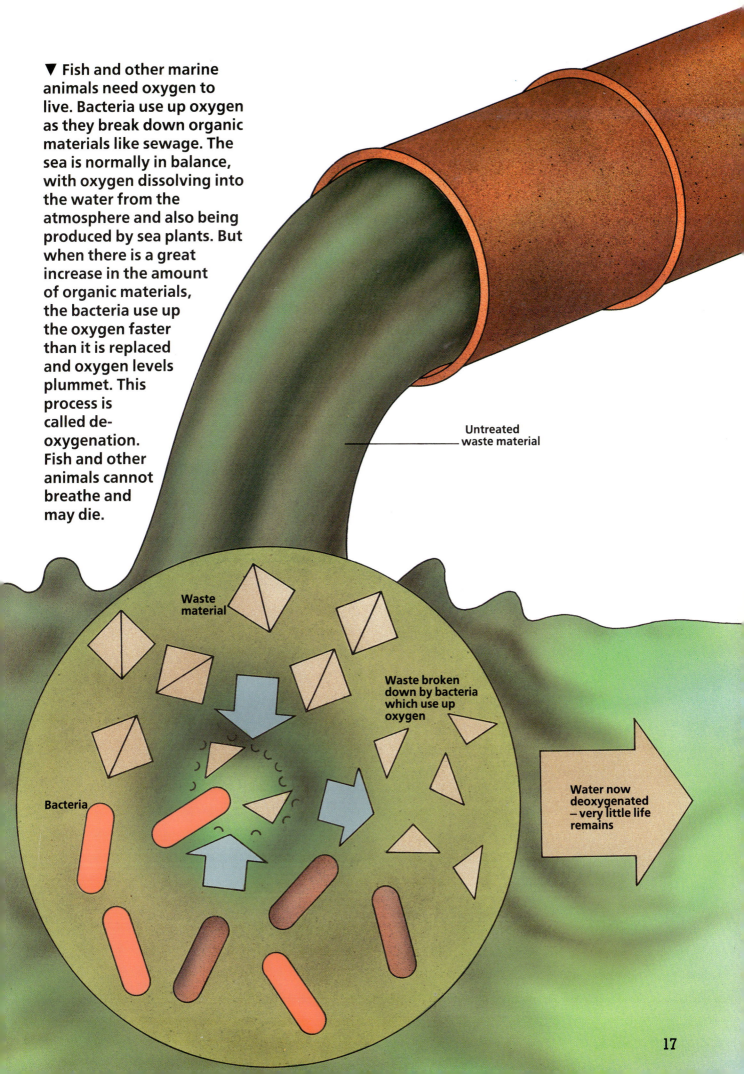

▼ Fish and other marine animals need oxygen to live. Bacteria use up oxygen as they break down organic materials like sewage. The sea is normally in balance, with oxygen dissolving into the water from the atmosphere and also being produced by sea plants. But when there is a great increase in the amount of organic materials, the bacteria use up the oxygen faster than it is replaced and oxygen levels plummet. This process is called de-oxygenation. Fish and other animals cannot breathe and may die.

Untreated waste material

Waste material

Waste broken down by bacteria which use up oxygen

Bacteria

Water now deoxygenated – very little life remains

17

METAL POLLUTION

Metals can be very poisonous pollutants although they occur naturally in the environment; blood, for example, contains iron. Metals get into the sea from volcanoes and forest fires, but also end up there as a result of human activities. Ocean dumping of some metals is illegal. However, along coastal areas with a lot of industry, metal pollution causes serious problems. Some industrial processes release metals into the air and water. Factory waste can carry metals. Chemicals used in farming also contain metals which can be washed into the sea by rivers and rain.

The level of metals in the sea is rising, and some of these metals can be very dangerous in large amounts. Copper, for example, is vital to many small marine animals, but when it was dumped off the Netherlands into the North Sea in 1965, the pollution killed all the plankton and fish in its path as it drifted up the coast. Also, animals retain metal if they consume it, and dangerous levels can build up in the food chain.

▼ The metal tin is used in TBT (tributyltin oxide), which is painted on boats' hulls to keep them free of barnacles. The tin slowly dissolves into the sea and has a serious effect on wildlife. Oysters, for example, suffer reduced growth and dog whelks become unable to breed. TBT is banned on small boats in many countries, but is still used on larger ships.

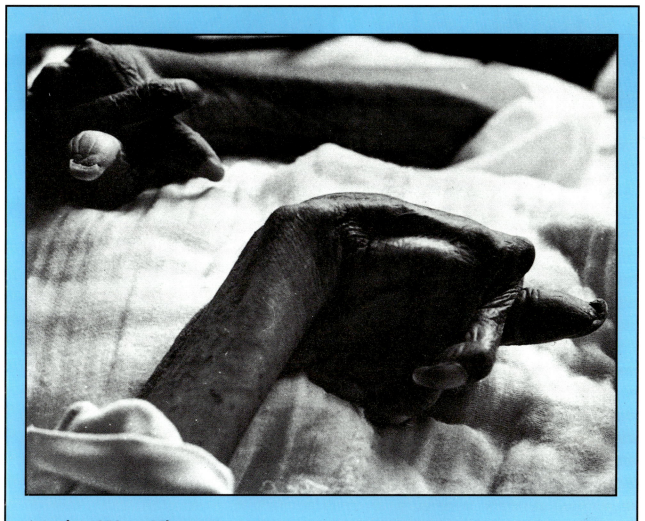

▲ In the 1950s at Minamata in Japan, mercury pollution entered the sea from a factory. The local people then ate the mercury-poisoned fish, with tragic consequences. Around 2,000 people were affected; some became crippled (above). Fishing was banned and eventually the pollution was stopped, but altogether at least 43 people died and 700 were left permanently affected.

► Mercury levels in white-tailed sea eagles, which feed on fish, have increased nine-fold during this century in Sweden and Finland. Mercury poisoning may be a factor in their decline.

CHEMICAL POISONS

A wide range of the artificial chemicals that we manufacture, including pesticides, end up in the sea. Many pesticides do not easily break down in the environment, so their levels are continually rising. Plants and animals may build up high levels of pesticides because they cannot eliminate them from their bodies.

Pesticides poison wildlife. The insecticide DDT can cause the shells of birds' eggs to be so thin that they break before they are ready to hatch. This especially affects fish-hunters, which are at the top of the food chain, when they eat fish that contain high levels of chemicals. DDT can also cause cancer. Its use has been banned in many countries since 1972, but its effects will remain in the environment for many years to come.

Among the huge numbers of other chemicals reaching the sea are detergents, acids and other industrial wastes and chemicals. Even though they are diluted by the sea, they can be harmful.

▼ Chemical pollution in the sea can have a variety of effects. The deaths of sea-birds at the Los Angeles Zoo in 1976 were blamed on the fish the birds were fed, which contained high levels of DDT. Deformities seen in ocean wildlife may be due to chemical pollution like PCBs; chemicals used in the electrical industry. It is believed this cormorant was born deformed as a result of PCB poisoning.

► The Rhine is a severely polluted river. By 1982, most of the species of fish that used to swim up it to breed had gone. Each year the Rhine receives over 300,000 tons of waste from cities that line its banks. The pollution does not just affect wildlife: about 20 million people get their drinking water from the Rhine. Much of the Rhine's pollution ends up in the North Sea.

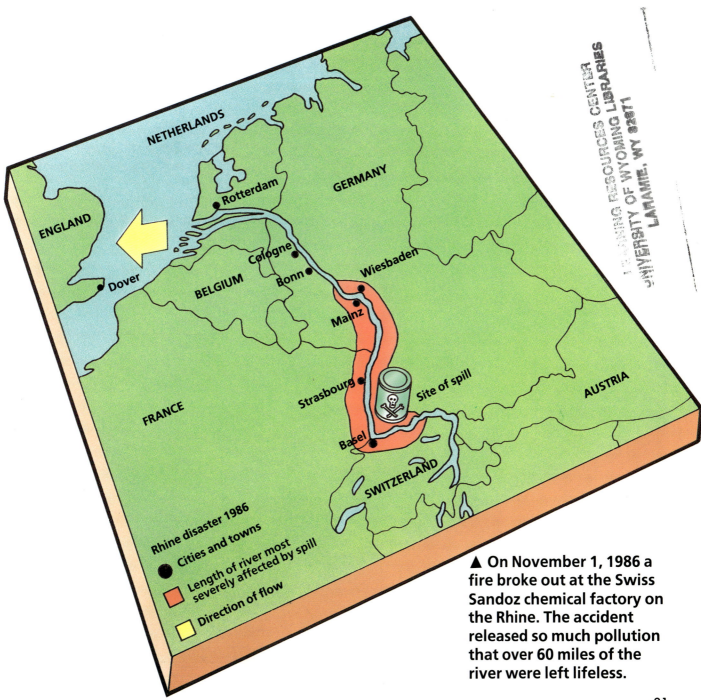

NETHERLANDS

GERMANY

Rotterdam

ENGLAND

Cologne

Wiesbaden

Dover

BELGIUM

Bonn

Mainz

FRANCE

Strasbourg

Site of spill

AUSTRIA

Basel

SWITZERLAND

Rhine disaster 1986

● Cities and towns

▬ Length of river most severely affected by spill

▯ Direction of flow

▲ On November 1, 1986 a fire broke out at the Swiss Sandoz chemical factory on the Rhine. The accident released so much pollution that over 60 miles of the river were left lifeless.

RADIOACTIVITY

Radioactivity consists of rays and particles given off by decaying atoms. It can be harmful to living things. Radioactivity occurs naturally in the sea at low levels, but the amount has increased due to human activity.

The nuclear bombs exploded in tests between the end of World War II and the early 1970s produced large amounts of radioactive dust, called fallout. The dust that was not immediately brought to the ground with rain was blasted high into the atmosphere where it still circles the Earth and gradually falls out of the sky, adding to the level of radioactivity.

Nuclear power stations use water for cooling during their normal operations and they discharge radioactive waste water into the ocean. Also, in the past, some radioactive waste was dumped at sea. Although this practice has now stopped, between 1967 and 1983 about 95,000 tons were dumped. Eventually the canisters will corrode and release radioactivity, although the levels are not likely to be high.

▼ **Worldwide there are about 600 submarines powered by nuclear energy. Normally they discharge a small amount of radioactivity which is spread throughout the sea so it has little effect. However, there is the risk of an accident which could expose the nuclear reactor which runs the submarine. This could lead to a large release of radioactivity in the area of the accident.**

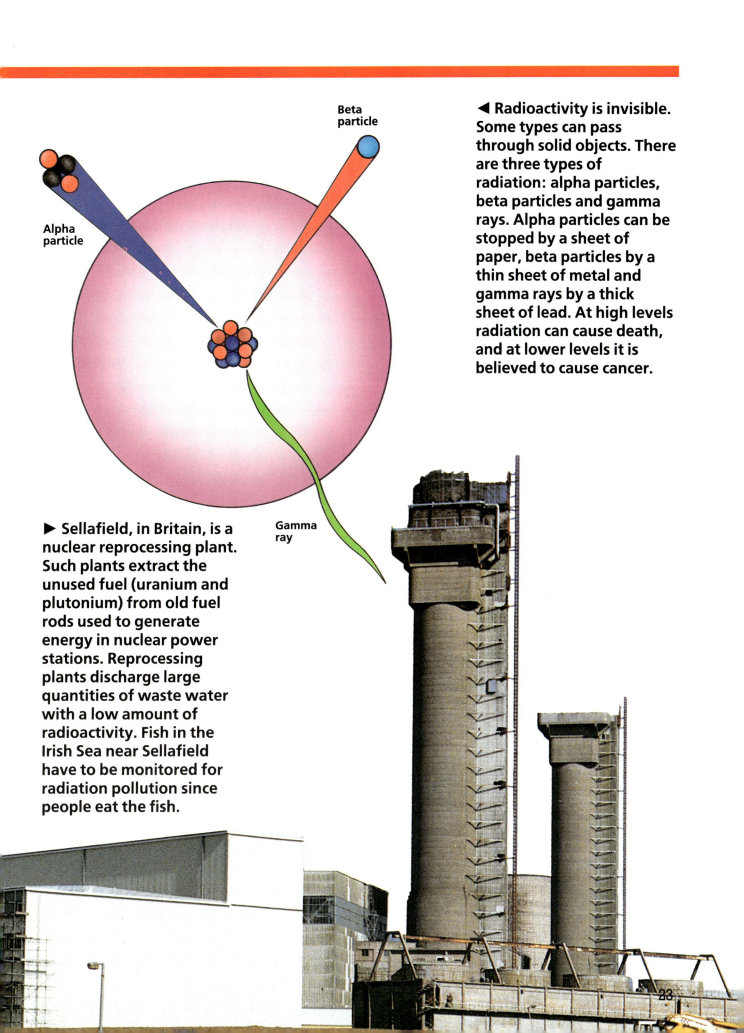

Beta particle

Alpha particle

Gamma ray

◄ Radioactivity is invisible. Some types can pass through solid objects. There are three types of radiation: alpha particles, beta particles and gamma rays. Alpha particles can be stopped by a sheet of paper, beta particles by a thin sheet of metal and gamma rays by a thick sheet of lead. At high levels radiation can cause death, and at lower levels it is believed to cause cancer.

► Sellafield, in Britain, is a nuclear reprocessing plant. Such plants extract the unused fuel (uranium and plutonium) from old fuel rods used to generate energy in nuclear power stations. Reprocessing plants discharge large quantities of waste water with a low amount of radioactivity. Fish in the Irish Sea near Sellafield have to be monitored for radiation pollution since people eat the fish.

◀ The Mediterranean Sea is almost completely surrounded by land. The time it takes to exchange all its water with the Atlantic is 70 years. The result is that pollution is not efficiently diluted; it is not replaced with clean water. So pollution builds up, mainly from industries like these on the Gibraltar coast.

The North Sea

Some 31 million people live around the North Sea and millions of visitors go there every summer. Every type of pollution gets into the North Sea. Much of the sewage from coastal towns is pumped untreated into the sea.

The Mediterranean

Tar balls, a type of oil pollution, are very frequent in the Mediterranean. Also, many coastal towns discharge untreated sewage into the sea.

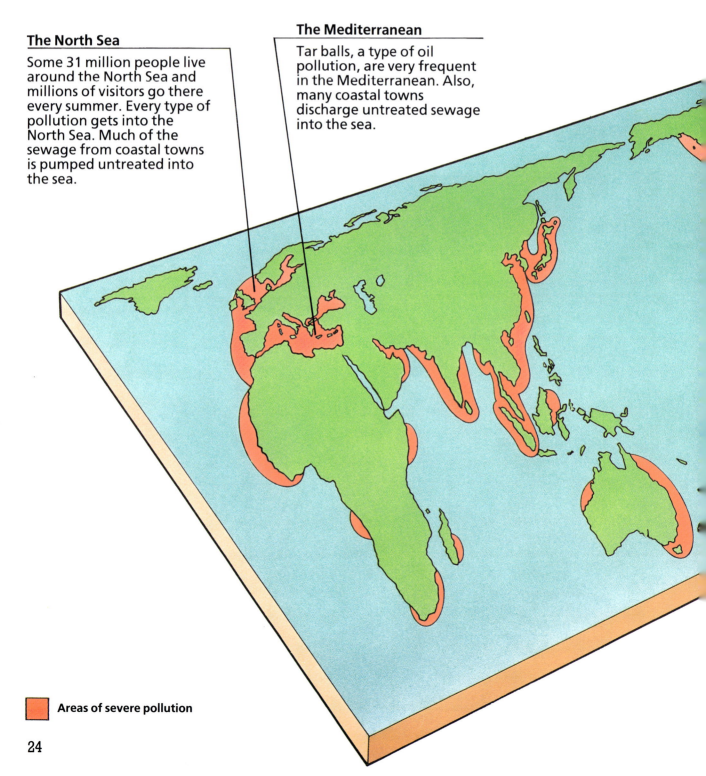

■ Areas of severe pollution

POLLUTION HOTSPOTS

Seas and oceans worldwide have been affected by pollution, particularly coastal waters. To change this we need increasing awareness among those who daily use the sea, as well as the general public, about the dangers to wildlife and people from sea pollution.

Factories must have rules on what and how much waste they drain into the ocean. This can be enforced by governments agreeing on strong pollution laws and by making polluters pay for the damage they cause. Governments can also ban industries from using pollutants until their effects are fully known. Most importantly, factories and power stations should produce a minimum amount of waste in the first place, use biodegradable products (which break down naturally) and attempt to recycle waste where possible. Sewage can be recycled to make fertilizer, for example. These steps would begin to tackle pollution problems.

The Caribbean and Gulf of Mexico

There is little coastal industrialization in this area, but pesticides from farming are washed into the Gulf. Also, serious local problems have occurred, including oil pollution at Galveston in Texas, mercury at Cartagena in Colombia and sewage at Port-au-Prince in Haiti.

The Atlantic coast of South America

Major cities along this seaboard include Recife and Rio de Janeiro in Brazil, and Buenos Aires in Argentina. These massive, expanding cities with their large populations and industrial activities are causing pollution problems in the western Atlantic.

The Pacific

The Pacific is the world's largest ocean. Some of its isolated islands have been used for nuclear weapons' testing in the past, and are now so radioactive that they have been declared unsafe for habitation for thousands of years.

WHAT YOU CAN DO

You can help solve some ocean pollution problems:
● Ask your parents to find out if they can recycle old engine oil locally instead of pouring it down the drain.
● Recycle garbage if you can, and break plastic six-pack holders before throwing them away. Do not drop litter off boats, or on beaches.
● Sewage, metal, pesticide, chemical and radioactive pollution problems can best be dealt with by local and national governments introducing legislation. You can help by writing to your politician to express concern.

Useful addresses

U.S. Environmental Protection Agency
401 M Street SW
Washington, D.C. 20460

Greenpeace
1436 U Street NW
Washington, D.C. 20009

Worldwatch Institute
1776 Massachusetts Avenue NW
Washington, D.C. 20036

Designing a poster:

One of the most important things that can be done is to make more people aware of the problem of ocean pollution. One way you can do this is to make a poster to hang up on a school bulletin board.

1) Think up a striking or clever heading for the poster that will grab the attention of the viewers.

2) Design an illustration or symbol like the one shown here or cut pictures out of magazines and make a collage that conveys the main message.

3) Read through this book and try to summarize in about 30-40 words what ocean pollution consists of and why it is a problem that affects everyone.

4) Again by reading through this book, make some suggestions as to what can be done to prevent further pollution of the planet's oceans and seas.

5) Include some other information if there is room, such as useful addresses to contact for more information about the problem or for campaign material.

1

2

3 **WILDLIFE AND PEOPLE DEPEND ON THE OCEAN; PARTICULARLY FOR FOOD. BUT WE ARE POISONING THIS FOOD SUPPLY WITH CHEMICALS, RADIOACTIVITY AND OTHER KINDS OF POLLUTION!**

WHAT CAN YOU DO?

4 •OILY WASTE FROM CARS CREATES POLLUTION IN THE SEA—DON'T DUMP OLD OIL IN THE STREET OR DOWN YOUR DRAIN.

•IF YOU GO TO THE BEACH MAKE SURE YOU DON'T LEAVE YOUR LITTER OR THROW IT INTO THE SEA.

5 •LITTER CAN KILL WILDLIFE IF THEY GET TRAPPED IN IT. TRY TO RECYCLE ALL METALS AND PLASTICS INSTEAD OF THROWING THEM AWAY.

USEFUL ADDRESSES

FACT FILE 1

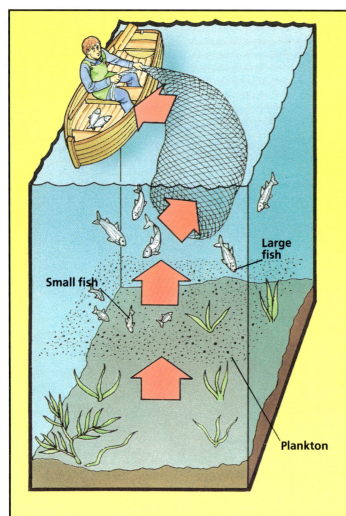

Large fish

Small fish

Plankton

Food chain
The food chain in the sea starts with plant plankton (which live in the surface waters where there is plenty of light), which are eaten by animal plankton. Small fish eat plankton and bigger fish eat the smaller fish. Seabirds and sea mammals feed on all fish. Some pollutants build up in animal and plant tissues. Animals at the top of the food chain eat animals that have pollutants in their bodies and can retain high levels of these pollutants.

Incinerating waste at sea
Waste incineration, burning waste at very high temperatures, has become frequent in recent years. Ocean incineration of PCBs at 2,192°F takes place in the North Sea in ships like the *Vulcanus* (below). Incineration is said to get rid of 99.9999 percent of the PCBs. However, partially-burned chemicals can escape from the incinerator smoke stacks and drift into the sea. These chemicals can be very toxic. Many nations have agreed to cut back or stop some types of ocean incineration in the 1990s.

Natural pollution

Many substances that we introduce to the sea as pollution can also get there naturally. Oil seeps into the sea in many coastal places. Oil is fossilized plant remains made up of chemicals called hydrocarbons. These are usually only harmful in the sea if concentrated in small areas.

Solid waste

Dredgers are ships which scoop up mud from the beds of rivers and seas. Like this one (right) in the Suez Canal, they keep waterways free for shipping. The solid waste they dredge up is often dumped at sea, smothering bottom-dwelling animals.

Politics and pollution

Protecting the seas from pollution depends on countries acting together. Countries around the North Sea and around the Mediterranean have met in recent years to work out ways in which they can clean up the seas which are their responsibility.

Public protests can pressure governments to obey rules decided at international conferences. This Greenpeace demonstration outside the North Sea conference in 1987 protested against ocean dumping of toxic waste.

FACT FILE 2

Beaches

Pollution of all kinds washes up on beaches. Many Mediterranean beaches are affected by oil pollution. One litter collection on a Texas beach found 15,600 six-pack holders in just three hours. One of the most disturbing kinds of ocean litter washed up on beaches is medical waste. In 1988, syringes, blood samples and infectious hospital waste were found on New York and New Jersey beaches (right). It was probably dumped illegally, perhaps by laboratories or health clinics.

Air pollution

Pollution rising into the air from factories and power stations, like those below on the west coast of England, falls to the sea in rain as solid particles or as gases, which dissolve in the surface water of the sea. It is very difficult to determine exactly how much sea pollution comes from the air because oceans are spread out over such a large area. However, scientists believe that the amount is large and contributes to ocean pollution. Around 3,000 tons of mercury a year, for example, are estimated to reach the sea from the burning of fossil fuels, especially coal.

GLOSSARY

Algal blooms – large concentrations of algae which grow excessively when the water is enriched with nutrients, by sewage dumping, for example. They can clog fishes' gills.

Biodegradable – substances which are biodegradable break down naturally in the environment.

DDT (dichlorodiphenoltrichloro-ethane) – a type of pesticide used in farming to kill insects. It breaks down in the environment very slowly and animals cannot get rid of it from their bodies. DDT is banned in many countries, but is still in wide use in poor countries.

Deoxygenation – the removal of oxygen from water. It occurs, for example, when large quantities of organic materials, like sewage, are dumped in the ocean. Bacteria which break down the organic material use up oxygen that fish and other animals need in order to survive.

Food chain – a sequence of living things that depend upon each other for food. Every living thing in the sea is dependent on the food chain, so if one species is affected by, for instance, pollution or overfishing, the whole chain can suffer.

Mercury – a metal which can damage both animals and people. It affects the nervous system, causing anxiety and headaches at low doses and convulsions, coma and death at higher levels. Mercury poisoning can also cause birth defects.

PCBs (polychlorinated biphenyls) – chemicals which are mostly used in electrical equipment. PCBs can kill marine animals or affect breeding by causing birth defects. PCB production has been cut back drastically since the dangers of these chemicals were discovered, but there are still large quantities of PCBs in old electrical equipment. PCBs break down very slowly in the environment.

Radioactivity – comes from the decay of unstable atoms. This process results in the production of tiny particles and sometimes rays. Some kinds of radioactivity are extremely damaging to living things and can stay dangerous for thousands of years.

TBT (tributyltin oxide) – a substance which contains the metal tin and is very toxic. It is used to paint the hulls of ships to keep them free of barnacles and other living things. It is lethal to a variety of ocean wildlife. Its use is banned in some countries.

INDEX

A
acids 20
air pollution 30
algal blooms 16, 31
Atlantic 25

B
bacteria 12, 16, 17
beaches 14, 16, 26, 30
beta particles 23
biodegradable 25, 31
boating 9

C
Caribbean 25
chemicals 5, 10, 11, 18, 20,
   21, 26, 28
coastal waters 25, 29
copper 18
coral reefs 6

D
DDT 20, 31
deoxygenation 17, 31
detergents 20
dredgers 29

E
Exxon Valdez 13

F
factories 11, 12, 18, 19,
   24, 25, 30
fallout 22
fertilizers 10, 11, 25
fish 6, 9, 13, 14, 17, 18, 23
fish farming 9

fishing nets 14, 15
food chain 18, 20, 28, 31
fossil fuels 9, 29, 30

G
Great Barrier Reef 6
Greenpeace 29
Gulf of Mexico 25

I
incineration 28
Indian Ocean 10
Irish Sea 23

L
litter 5, 11, 14-15, 26, 30

M
medical waste 30
Mediterranean 24, 29, 30
mercury 19, 25, 30, 31
metal 18, 19, 26
Minamata 19

N
natural pollution 29
North Sea 16, 18, 21, 24,
   28, 29
nuclear bombs 22, 25
nuclear power stations
   22, 23
nuclear submarines 22

O
oil 5, 9, 12, 13, 24-26, 29,
   30
oil slicks 5, 11-13

oil tankers 12
oxygen 6, 16, 17

P
Pacific Ocean 5, 25
parasites 16
PCBs 20, 28, 31
pesticides 5, 10, 11, 20, 25
plankton 5, 6, 18, 28
plastic 5, 14, 26

R
radioactivity 5, 11, 22, 23,
   25, 26, 31
rain 6, 18, 30
recycling 12, 15, 25, 26
reprocessing plants 23
Rhine 21
rivers 10-12, 18

S
Sandoz factory 21
Sellafield 23
sewage 5, 10, 11, 16-18,
   21, 24-26
ships 11, 14, 18
solid waste 29
Suez Canal 29

T
tar balls 24
TBT (tributyltin oxide) 18,
   31

W
wildlife, damage to
   13-16, 18, 20

Photographic Credits:
Cover and pages 21, 22 and 30 top: Frank Spooner Pictures; page 4-5: Science Photo Library; page 6, 9, 10 and 15 middle: Plant Earth Pictures; pages 6-7, 11, 14 left and 30 bottom: the Environmental Picture Library; pages 8, 9,top inset, 15 bottom and 18: Robert Harding Picture Library; pages 13 top and bottom, 20 and 23: Topham Picture Library; pages 14-15 and 29 top: Spectrum Photo Library; pages 15 top and 19 bottom: Bruce Coleman Photo Library; pages 16, 24, 28 and 29 bottom: Greenpeace; page 19 top: Magnum Photos.